Music by Women for Study and Analysis

Joseph N. Straus
Queens College and the Graduate School
City University of New York

Prentice Hall
Englewood Cliffs, New Jersey 07632

Library of Congress Cataloging-in-Publication Data

Music by women for study and analysis / [edited by] Joseph N. Straus.
    p. of music.
    Includes indexes.
    ISBN 0-13-093071-7
    1. Musical analysis--Music collections. 2. Harmony. 3. Women
composers' music. I. Straus, Joseph Nathan.
MT6.5.M84 1993   92-43643
                                                        CIP
                                                         M

Editorial/production supervision and interior design: Jordan Ochs
Acquisitions editor: Bud Therien
Editorial assistant: Lee Mamunes
Prepress buyer: Herb Klein
Manufacturing buyer: Robert Anderson
Cover design: Lucille Paccione

 © 1993 by Joseph N. Straus

Printed in the United States of America
10 9 8 7 6 5 4 3 2 1

ISBN   0-13-093071-7

Prentice-Hall International (UK) Limited, *London*
Prentice-Hall of Australia Pty. Limited, *Sydney*
Prentice-Hall Canada Inc., *Toronto*
Prentice-Hall Hispanoamericana, S.A., *Mexico*
Prentice-Hall of India Private Limited, *New Delhi*
Prentice-Hall of Japan, Inc., *Tokyo*
Simon & Schuster Asia Pte. Ltd., *Singapore*
Editora Prentice-Hall do Brasil, Ltda., *Rio de Janeiro*

Contents

Preface

This is an anthology of music by women organized to illustrate the standard topics in first- and second-year harmony courses, from root-position chords through augmented sixth chords. In virtually all current textbooks and anthologies, the musical illustrations are exclusively by men. This anthology is designed to redress that imbalance and thus to give students and teachers of music a more complete understanding of the history and range of their art.

This anthology contains 102 musical excerpts by nineteen composers, representing a variety of nationalities and historical periods. All the excerpts have been selected for their intrinsic beauty and their aptness in illustrating the theoretical topic at hand. Within each section of the anthology, the excerpts are arranged in roughly ascending order of pedagogical difficulty but, of course, it is impossible to be precise about this. Readers interested in specific topics or composers should consult the two indexes at the end of the book.

Although this anthology contains only excerpts, most of the works represented are both published and recorded. It is our hope that students and teachers, who have their first contact with a piece because it illustrates some theoretical topic they are studying, will be inspired to learn the piece as a whole, and will thus be drawn into the rich and varied subculture of music by women composers.

This anthology is not the work of a single person or small group, but rather of a large community of musicians, both students and teachers, who share an interest in bringing a remarkable and important repertoire to the attention of all musicians. It began as an initiative of the Committee on the Status of Women of the Society for Music Theory, chaired by Judith Lochhead, and the members of that committee, past and present, have participated actively in producing it. In the early stages of the project, the following scholars assisted in choosing the works to be included: Adrienne Fried Block, Rae Linda Brown, Karin Pendle, Nancy Reich, Catherine Smith, Ruth Solie, and Elizabeth Wood. The task of selecting appropriate excerpts fell to Scott Brickman, Kathryn Bosi, Steven Bruns, Maureen Carr, Lisa Fishman, Sheila Forrester, Michele Fromson, Douglass Green, Anne Hall, Lori Hallam, Ellie Hisama, Alexis Johnson, Elizabeth Keathley, Marianne Kielian-Gilbert, Judith Lochhead, Elizabeth Marvin (and students in the Eastman School of Music's Pedagogy of Theory Class, Spring 1991), Charles Morrison, Jennifer Shaw, Lisa Shirah, Catherine Smith, Deborah Stein, and Linda Swedensky. Song texts were translated by Allan Atlas (Italian), Halina Goldberg (Polish), Ruth Koizim (French), and Hedi Siegel (German). Performing editions of music by Barbara Strozzi were prepared by Kathryn Bosi and Michele Fromson. Frank Samarotto expertly transcribed the excerpts by Leonarda and Strozzi. At a late stage, Claire Boge, Drora Pershing, and Mary Wennerstrom reviewed the manuscript and made extensive suggestions for revision. They made an extraordinarily generous commitment of their time and expertise, and shaped this anthology very much for the better. For advice on matters contractual, editorial, and otherwise, Sally Goldfarb has my deep and continuing gratitude.

Joseph N. Straus
Brooklyn, New York

1 Diatonic Chords in 5/3 Position (Root Position)

1. Louise Reichardt, "Kriegslied des Mays" ("War Song of May"), mm. 1–4

When springtime's sentries go on duty, and the lark briskly sounds the drumroll.

2. Louise Reichardt, "Frühlingsblumen" ("Spring Flowers")

The joyous summertime truly fills me with happiness; It renews my blood, May rejoices in delight; The lark flies
upward with its bright call; The birds sing beautifully along with the nightingale.

3. Louise Reichardt, "Der Sänger geht" ("The Singer Walks"), mm. 1–10

The singer walks on rocky paths, tears his clothes on thorns; He must wade through river and swamps, and no one extends a helping hand.

4. Elizabeth Jacquet de la Guerre, Suite in D Minor, second Rigaudon

5. Isabella Leonarda, Kyrie, from *Messa Prima*, mm. 1–3

Lord have mercy on us.

6. Amy Marcy Cheney Beach, Symphony in E Minor, Op. 32 ("Gaelic"), third movement, mm. 25–27   [Lento con molto espressione (♩ = 72)]

7. Clara Wieck Schumann, "Le Ballet des Revenants" ("The Dance of the Ghosts"), from *Quatre pièces Caractéristiques*, Op. 5, No. 4, mm. 44–67

[Allegro ma non troppo]

2 Diatonic Chords in 6/3 Position (First Inversion)

8. Barbara Strozzi, "Or che Apollo," from *Arie a voce sola*, Op. 8, mm. 66–68

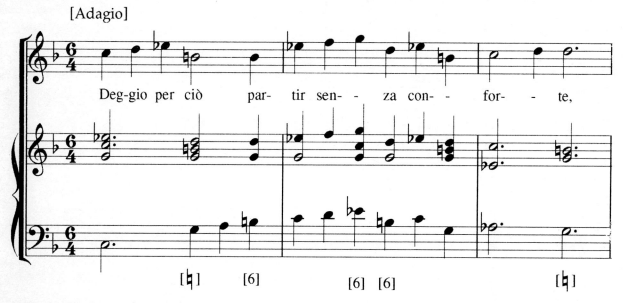

I must therefore leave without comfort.

9. Elizabeth Jacquet de la Guerre, Suite in A Minor, Sarabande, mm. 1–8

10. Marianne Martinez, Sonata in A Major, first movement, mm. 1–3

11. Josephine Lang, "Mag da draussen Schnee sich thürmen" ("Let the snow pile up outside"), mm. 1–5

12. Louise Reichardt, "Aus Ariels Offenbarungen" ("From Ariel's Revelation"), mm. 1–17

Lily, look at me! You sparkle with dew; you are sad, in you I sense suffering! I am happy, Rose, greet me! You smell heavenly, in you I sense joy.

13. Pauline Viardot-Garcia, "Les Cavaliers" ("The Horsemen"), mm. 20–27

My sister, did you see those two horsemen? The ones who just passed on their black chargers? Never did a prince or the son of a queen have such supreme grace!

14. Josephine Lang, "Gott sei mir Sünder gnädig" ("God, be merciful to me, a sinner"), mm. 5–10

Even when burdens oppress, even then you will be exalted!

15. Clara Wieck Schumann, "Ich stand in dunklen Träumen" ("I stood in dark dreams"), from Six Songs, Op. 13, No. 1, mm. 28–37

And ah, I cannot believe that I have lost you!

16. Fanny Mendelssohn Hensel, "O Traum der Jugend, O goldner Stern" ("O Dream of Youth, O Golden Star"), mm. 1–15

3 Diatonic Chords in 6/4 Position (Second Inversion)

17. Louise Reichardt, "Poesie von Tieck" ("A Poem by Tieck"), mm. 1–10

Rest easy my sweetheart in the shade of the green twilight; The grass rustles in the meadows, the shade fans and cools you, and true love reigns.

18. Clara Wieck Schumann, "Caprice à la Boléro," from *Quatre Pièces Caractéristiques*, **Op. 5,**
   No. 2, mm. 1–13

19. Fanny Mendelssohn Hensel, "Du bist die Ruh" ("You are tranquility"), from *Six Songs*, Op. 7, No. 4, mm. 25–32   [Moderato assai]

All that my eye encompasses is illuminated by your radiance alone. O fill it completely.

20. Josephine Lang, "Ich gab dem Schicksal dich zurück" ("I gave you back to your fate"), mm. 83–95

O, you don't know what I bury with your portrait!

21. Fanny Mendelssohn Hensel, No. 11 from *Selected Piano Works*, mm. 1–17

Allegro vivace

22. Amy Marcy Cheney Beach, Symphony in E Minor, Op. 32 ("Gaelic"), second movement, mm. 1–8

23. Josephine Lang, "Ob ich manchmal Dein gedenke" ("Do I sometimes think of you?"), mm. 25–36

[Langsam und Ausdrucksvoll]

Dich zu lie - ben   ist mein sein!   Dich zu lie - ben

ist mein sein!

To love you is my existence!

24. Mary Carr Moore, "O Wond'rous Soul," Op. 79, No. 9, mm. 1–7

4 Seventh Chords

25. Louise Reichardt, "Die Blume der Blumen" ("The Flower of Flowers"), mm. 1–10

A beautiful flower blooms in a distant land; It is such a heavenly creation known only to a few.

26. Louise Reichardt, "Buss Lied," ("Song of Repentence"), mm. 19–26

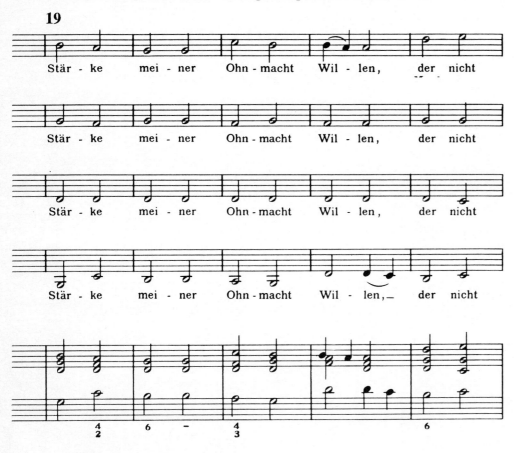

Fortify my weak resolve which is powerless without you.

27. Josephine Lang, "In weite Ferne" ("In the distant realm"), mm. 1–7

In the distant realm I wish to dream! There where you dwell.

28. Josephine Lang, ''Ich liebe dich und will dich ewig lieben'' (''I love you and want to love you forever''), mm. 1–14

I want to renew my vows to you, and all the gods on high shall hear me.

29. Josephine Lang, "Ob ich manchmal Dein gedenke" ("Do I sometimes think of you?"), mm. 1–4

Do I sometimes think of you? If only you knew how much I do!

30. Amy Marcy Cheney Beach, "Menuet Italien," from *Three Pieces*, Op. 28, No. 2, mm. 1–9

Allegretto con delicatezza.

31. Amy Marcy Cheney Beach, Barcarolle, from *Three Pieces*, Op. 28, No. 1, mm. 1–10

32. Clara Wieck Schumann, Trio in G Minor for Violin, Cello, and Piano, Op. 17, first movement, mm. 1–9 and 265–287

33. Clara Wieck Schumann, "Le Ballet des Revenants" ("The Dance of the Ghosts"), from *Quatre Pièces Caractéristiques*, **Op. 5, No. 4, mm. 5–12**

34. Alma Schindler Mahler, "Hymne," from *Five Songs* (1924), mm. 9–16 [Ganz ruhig beginnend, mit freiem Vortag]

The holy communion's divine meaning is a mystery to the earthly senses.

35. Florence Price, "Sympathy," mm. 11–20 [Andantino]

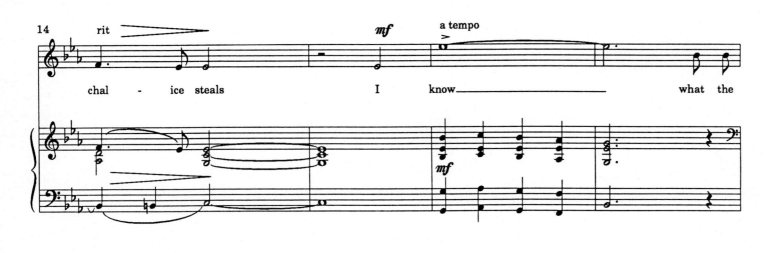

chal - ice steals   I   know _____ what the

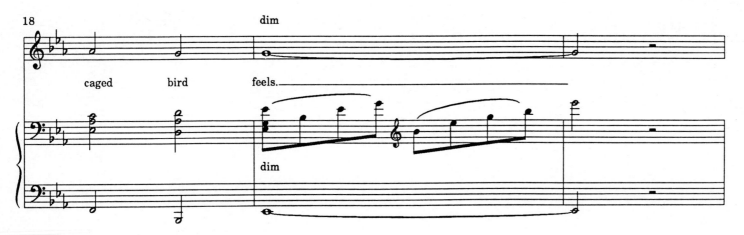

caged   bird   feels. _____

36. Fanny Mendelssohn Hensel, "Notturno," from *Selected Piano Works*, No. 5, mm. 1–12

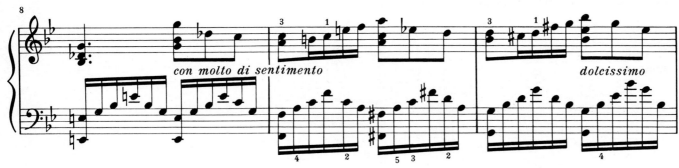

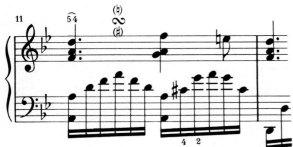

*) Change pedal with every change of harmony
   (composer's note).

37. Elizabeth Jacquet de la Guerre, Suite in D Minor, Sarabande, mm. 21–28

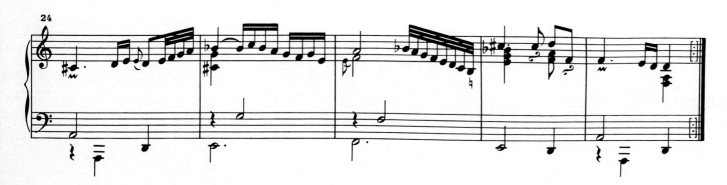

5 Ninth Chords

38. Clara Wieck Schumann, Ballade, from *Vier Stücke aus Soirées Musicales*, **Op. 6, No. 4, mm. 58–70**

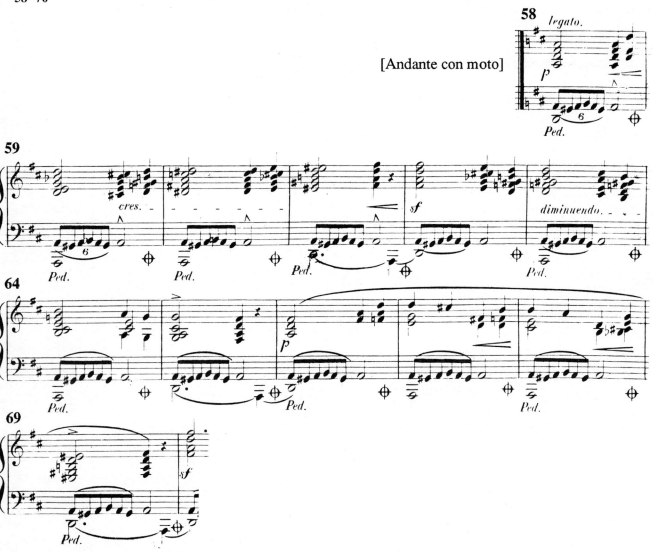

39. Clara Wieck Schumann, *Trois Romances*, Op. 11, No. 2, mm. 41–50

40. Amy Marcy Cheney Beach, "Meadow-Larks," Op. 79, No. 1, mm. 17–21 [Allegro vivace]

41. Alma Schindler Mahler, "In meines Vaters Garten" ("In my father's garden"), from *Five Songs* (1910), No. 2, mm. 126–129

There stands a sun-drenched apple tree.

42. Mary Carr Moore, *David Rizzio*, Op. 89, Act 1, mm. 1–19

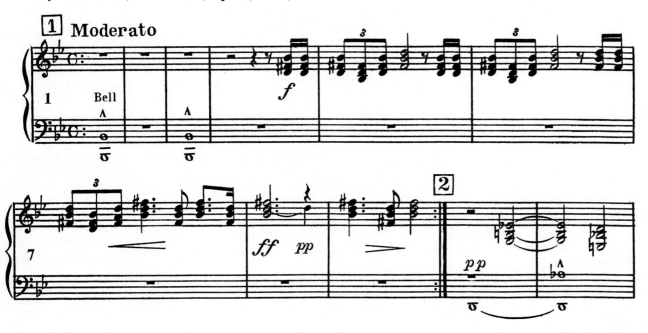

3 CHORUS. (Off Stage)

Small Organ, Off Stage.

51

43. Nadia Boulanger, "J'ai frappé" ("I knocked"), mm. 1–5

My hand knocked at the closed door, And other hands responded from a distance.

6 Applied (Secondary) Chords

44. Maria Wolowska Szymanowska, Nocturne, mm. 1–5

45. Louise Reichardt, "Unruhiger Schlaf" ("Restless sleep"), mm. 1–26

The cherry tree blooms, I sit here in silence; The blossom falls and touches my lips; The moon also falls into the earth's lap, and looks so bright, so red and large! The stars twinkle mysteriously in the firmament, and will not suffer our gaze!

46. Amy Marcy Cheney Beach, "In Autumn," from *Sketches*, Op. 15, No. 1, mm. 39–55

A. P. S. 2870

47. Alma Schindler Mahler, "Ich wandle unter Blumen" ("I wander among flowers"), from *Five Songs* (1910), No. 5, mm. 1–8

I wander among flowers and am myself in bloom; I wander as if in a dream and sway with every step.

48. Josephine Lang, "Wenn zwei von einander scheiden" ("When two people part"), mm. 1–8

When two people part, they shake hands.

49. Pauline Viardot-Garcia, "Die Soldatenbraut" ("The Soldier's Bride"), mm. 20–26 [Tempo di marcia]

My darling will never be a general — if only they would give him his discharge.

50. Alma Schindler Mahler, "Bei dir ist es traut" ("It is cozy here with you"), from Five Songs (1910), No. 4, mm. 29–41

Let us be quiet, then no one will suspect we are here!

51. Louise Reichardt, "Tiefe Andacht" ("Deep devotion"), from *Sechs geistliche Lieder*, mm. 40–44

Promise to us, you are silenced. Adoration, glory, and thanks to you!

52. Clara Wieck Schumann, "Das ist ein Tag, der klingen mag" ("This is a day that will resound"), from Six Songs from *Jucunde*, Op. 23, No. 5, mm. 28–45   [Lebhaft]

das ist____ ein Früh-lings-lied, das ist ein

Früh___lings_lied.

The echo reverberates, It rings and sings everywhere, This is a song of spring.

53. Clara Wieck Schumann, Trio in G Minor for Violin, Cello, and Piano, Op. 17, second movement, mm. 154–68

54. Amy Marcy Cheney Beach, Quintet in F-sharp Minor for Piano and Strings, Op. 67, second movement, mm. 1–9 (piano tacet)

7 Modulation

55. Clara Wieck Schumann, "Ich stand in dunklen Träumen" ("I stood in dark dreams"), from Six Songs, Op. 13, No. 1, mm. 1–13

Ich stand in dunklen Träu_men und starr_te ihr Bildniss '

9

an, und das gelieb _ te Ant _ litz heimlich zu le _ ben be_

cresc.

13

gann.

I stood in dark dreams and gazed at her portrait, And the beloved features mysteriously came to life.

56. Fanny Mendelssohn Hensel, "Schwanenlied" ("Swan Song"), from *Six Songs*, Op. 1, No. 1, mm. 1–17

A star came falling down from its glittering height, This is the star of love that I see falling there.

57. Elizabeth Jacquet de la Guerre, Suite in F Major, Allemande, mm. 1–7

58. Elizabeth Jacquet de la Guerre, Suite in A Minor, Allemande, mm. 1–8

59. Isabella Leonarda, Credo from *Messa Prima*, mm. 78–96

93

C.
sus et se_____ pul - tus est.

T.
_____ sus et se_____ pul - tus est.

4 ♯3   ♯   [4   ♯3]   ♯

He was crucified also for us, suffered under Pontius Pilate, and was buried.

60. Fanny Mendelssohn Hensel, "Nachtwanderer" ("Night Wanderer"), from *Six Songs*, Op. 7, No. 1, mm. 1–17

I wander through the silent night, while the moon stalks in secret silence, often emerging from the mantle of dark clouds; And here and there in the valley, the nightingale awakens; then everything is grey again, grey and silent.

61. Louise Reichardt, "Ida," mm. 1–26

When I am dead, put me in a little boat; Set it on fire, so that I am completely consumed. Free the boat from its moorings, and sing this little verse: Heymdal, when I lived, you never loved me.

62. Maria Wołowska Szymanowska, Ballada, mm. 1–12

1. O - na mu z ko - sza da - je ma - li - ny, a on jej kwia - tki do wian - ka,

Who is the handsome youth? Who is the maiden with him? They walk in the moonlight along the bank of Lake Svitez with its livid waters. She gives him raspberries from her basket and he gives her little flowers for the garland in her hair.

63. Alma Schindler Mahler, "Die stille Stadt" ("The silent city"), from *Five Songs* (1910), No. 1, mm. 1–5

There is a city in the valley, a pale day is over.

64. Fanny Mendelssohn Hensel, "Bitte" ("A Plea"), from *Six Songs*, Op. 7, No. 5

Weil auf mir du dunk_les Au_ge, ü _ be   dei _ ne gan_ze
Nimm mit dei_nem Zau_ber_dun_kel die _ se   Welt von hin_nen

Macht,   ern_ste mil_de träu_me_rei_che un_er_gründlich sü_sse
mir,   dass du ü _ ber mei_nem Le_ben ein_sam schwebest für und

Gaze on me for a while you dark eye, bring your full power into play, earnest, gentle, dreamy, unfathomable sweet night. Take with your magic darkness this world away from me, that over my life you alone shall hover for ever and for ever.

8 Linear Progressions and Sequences

65. Clara Wieck Schumann, "Caprice à la Boléro," from *Quatre Pièces Caractéristiques*, Op. 5, No. 2, mm. 149–159

66. Amy Marcy Cheney Beach, "A Hermit Thrush at Eve," Op. 92, No. 1, mm. 10–17

67. Alma Schindler Mahler, "Der Erkennende" ("The Wise One"), from *Five Songs* (1924), No. 3, mm. 1–11

People love us, and in sadness they rise from the dinner table, and leave to cry for us.

68. Barbara Strozzi, "Dessistete omai, pensiere" ("Cease now, thoughts") from *Ariette a voce sola*, **Op. 6, mm. 34–45**

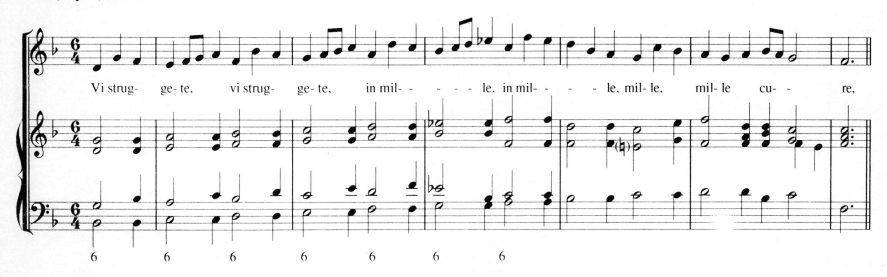

There you struggle in thousands of woes.

69. Cécile Chaminade, Sonata in C Minor, Op. 21, first movement, mm. 43–57

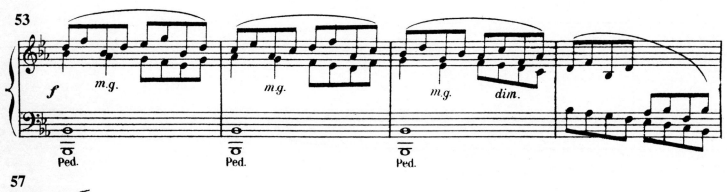

70. Lily Boulanger, "Au pied de mon lit" ("At the foot of my bed"), from *Clairières dans le ciel*, (Clearing in the Sky), No. 5, mm. 1–6

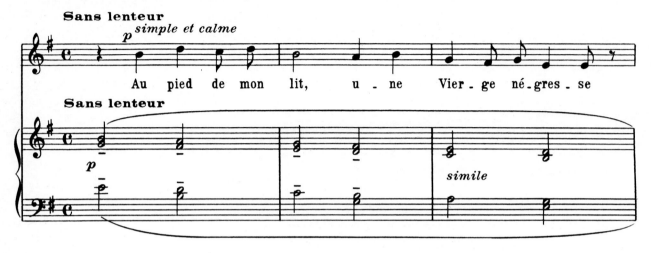

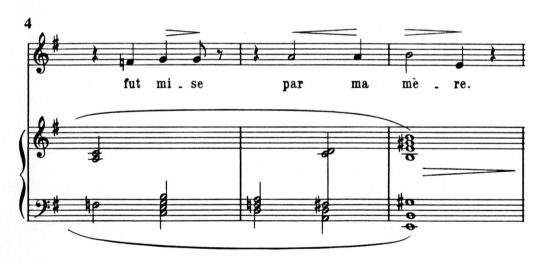

At the foot of my bed, a black Virgin was placed by my mother.

71. Elizabeth Jacquet de la Guerre, Suite in D Minor, second Gigue, mm. 13–25

72. Marianne Martinez, Sonata in E Major, first movement, mm. 63–78

73. Maria Wolowska Szymanowska, Etude in D Minor, mm. 1–9

74. Florence Price, Sonata in E Minor, first movement, mm. 103–113 [Allegro]

9 ♭II (Neapolitan)

75. Amy Marcy Cheney Beach, "Phantoms," from *Sketches*, Op. 15, No. 2, mm. 17–33

[Allegretto scherzando]

76. Josephine Lang, "Ich gab dem Schicksal dich zurück" ("I gave you back to your fate"), mm. 53–68 [Larghetto espressivo]

It is a wondrous feeling that forever cripples the heart, When we experience our first disappointment—A feeling that we never get over.

77. Clara Wieck Schumann, *Trois Romances,* **Op. 11, No. 2, mm. 136–151** [Andante]

78. Clara Wieck Schumann, "Impromptu—Le Sabbat," from *Quatre Pièces Caractéristiques*, **Op. 5, No. 1, mm. 105–116**

[Allegro furioso]

107

112

79. Fanny Mendelssohn Hensel, No. 3 from *Selected Piano Works*, mm. 57–63

10 Augmented Triads

80. Clara Wieck Schumann, Notturno, from *Vier Stücke aus Soirées Musicales*, Op. 6, No. 2, mm. 1–10 and 112–126

81. Alma Schindler Mahler, "Ekstase" ("Ecstasy"), from *Five Songs* (1924), No. 2, mm. 8–23

And your wonders lie before me like meadows in May on which the sun shines.

82. Ethel Smyth, *The Wreckers*, Act I, seven measures at rehearsal no. 32

83. Florence Price, "Hold Fast to Dreams," mm. 22–26

[Tempo Moderato]

84. Cécile Chaminade, "Rêve d'un soir" ("Dream of an evening"), mm. 3–6

Dream of an evening, dream of an hour, you fled on the wings of desire.

11 Augmented Sixth Chords

85. Fanny Mendelssohn Hensel, "Abschied von Rom" ("Departure from Rome"), from *Selected Piano Works*, **No. 6, mm. 1–3**

86. Fanny Mendelssohn Hensel, Trio for Violin, Cello, and Piano, Op. 11, first movement, mm. 345–358

87. Mary Carr Moore, Sonata for Violin (or Flute) and Piano, Op. 81, No. 6, first movement, mm. 1–12

88. Josephine Lang, "Immer sich rein" ("Always rejoicing"), mm. 13–18

Hopping and jumping, what bliss to do it!

89. Maria Wolowska Szymanowska, Etude in E Major, mm. 1–9

90. Amy Marcy Cheney Beach, "Ah Love, but a day," from *Three Browning Songs*, **Op. 44, No. 2, mm. 11–19**

Sum - mer has stopped,_____ Sum - mer has

stopped.

91. Amy Marcy Cheney Beach, "Meadow-Larks," Op. 79, No. 1, mm. 29–38

92. Margaret Bonds, "Troubled Water," mm. 9–24 [Allegro ($\quarternote = 138$)]

93. Clara Wieck Schumann, "Ballade," from *Vier Stücke aus Soirées Musicales*, **Op. 6, No. 4,**
mm. 24–39 [Allegro con moto]

12 Common Tone Augmented Sixth and Diminished Seventh Chords

94. Fanny Mendelssohn Hensel, No. 11 from *Selected Piano Works*, mm. 72–86

95. Mary Carr Moore, *David Rizzio*, Act I, seven measures at rehearsal no. 37

96. Alma Schindler Mahler, "In meines Vaters Garten" ("In my father's garden"), from *Five Songs* (1910), No. 2, mm. 36–42

The very youngest beauty—Bloom my heart, blossom!

97. Josephine Lang, "Fee'n-Reigen" ("The Dance of the Fairies"), mm. 18–28

The silvery bells of the lily of the valley, they ring for the dance!

98. Amy Marcy Cheney Beach, "In Autumn," from *Sketches*, Op. 15, No. 1, mm. 1–8

13 Enharmonic Reinterpretation of Augmented Sixth and Diminished Seventh Chords

99. Marcy Cheney Beach, Symphony in E Minor, Op. 32 ("Gaelic"), third movement, mm. 16–20

100. Amy Marcy Cheney Beach, "A Hermit Thrush at Morn," Op. 92, No. 2, mm. 37–43

101. Fanny Mendelssohn Hensel, Trio for Piano, Violin, and Cello, Op. 11, first movement, mm. 381–400

102. Clara Wieck Schumann, *Trois Romances*, Op. 11, No. 3, mm. 1–24

Index of Composers and Works

Index of Topics